M000202003

ISBN: 978-1-4300-3499-5

Item: 005680981

Dewey Decimal Classification Number: 231.7

Subject Heading: GOD \ BIBLE. O.T. PSALMS \ CHRISTIAN LIFE

Eric Geiger
Vice President, Church Resources

Ronnie Floyd
General Editor

David Francis
Managing Editor

Gena Rogers
Sam O'Neal
Content Editors

Philip Nation
Director, Adult Ministry Publishing

Faith Whatley
Director, Adult Ministry

Send questions/comments to: Content Editor, *Bible Studies for Life: Adults*, One LifeWay Plaza, Nashville, TN 37234-0175; or make comments on the Web at *www.BibleStudiesforLife.com*

Printed in the United States of America

For ordering or inquiries, visit www.lifeway.com; write LifeWay Small Groups; One LifeWay Plaza; Nashville, TN 37234-0152; or call toll free (800) 458-2772.

Social Media

Connect with a community of *Bible Studies for Life* users. Post responses to questions, share teaching ideas, and link to great blog content. *Facebook.com/BibleStudiesForLife*

Get instant updates about new articles, giveaways, and more. **@BibleMeetsLife**

The App

Simple and straightforward, this elegantly designed iPhone app gives you all the content of the Small Group Member Book—plus a whole lot more—right at your fingertips. Available in the iTunes App Store; search **"Bible Studies for Life."**

Blog

At ***BibleStudiesForLife.com/blog*** you will find all the magazine articles we mention in this study guide and music downloads provided by LifeWay Worship. Plus, leaders and group members alike will benefit from the blog posts written for people in every life stage—singles, parents, boomers, and senior adults—as well as media clips, connections between our study topics, current events, and much more.

Training

For helps on how to use Bible Studies for Life, tips on how to better lead groups, or additional ideas for leading this session, visit: ***www.ministrygrid.com/web/biblestudiesforlife.***

Storms are coming. Find shelter.

Hardly a day goes by that I don't check the weather app on my phone. Why? Because I want to know what I might face today. I want to be prepared for sunshine or rain, powdery snow or ice on the roads, clear skies or a tornado.

I wish I had an app that would give me a different kind of forecast. I need an app that will give me the forecast for the real storms of my life—the storms in relationships, temptations, trouble at work, and the general chaos of the daily grind. Unfortunately, no such app exists. Instead, we typically put one foot in front of the other and slog through each day as it comes.

But we don't have to live that way.

We know two things for sure about the storms of life:

1. Storms are going to happen.

2. We're never alone, even when life assaults us with all of its brutality.

I'm glad you're taking this journey with me as we study a few psalms—ancient worship songs—to learn where God is and what God is doing in the middle of our storms. At times we may feel like asking, "Where is God when life is hard?" There are important answers to that question, as the psalms will help us see. But this study offers more than just information about God. *Storm Shelter* will also help you answer the question, "Where do I go when life gets tough?"

Let's learn to live in the middle of the ancient lyrics, these wonderful psalms. Let's encounter the truth that God does show up personally in our lives, no matter what storm comes our way. He is our storm shelter.

Philip Nation

Philip Nation is the director of Adult Ministry Publishing at LifeWay and serves as the teaching pastor for The Fellowship, a multi-campus church in Nashville, Tennessee. He coauthored *Compelled: Living the Mission of God* and *Transformational Discipleship: How People Really Grow* along with serving as the general editor for *The Mission of God Study Bible*. Read more from Philip at *PhilipNation.net*.

contents

SESSION 1

THE SHELTER OF GOD'S PRESENCE

What is the biggest storm you've ever encountered?

#BSFLpresence

QUESTION #1

God is with me no matter what I'm facing.

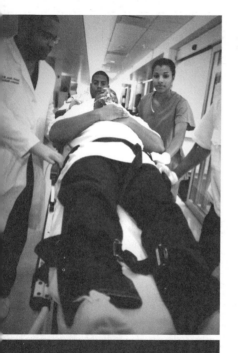

THE BIBLE MEETS LIFE

I knew what I wanted to say, but my mouth wouldn't cooperate. I thought: *Why am I so tongue-tied? I must be tired.* But after trying again to answer my wife's question, I found I was physically speechless. After a few frantic moments, the paramedics were called. It was all a blur from there. Sirens. Wheeling through the emergency room. Getting a CAT scan of my brain.

The diagnosis was a transient ischemic attack (TIA), often called a "mini-stroke." There's nothing quite like being 41 years old and hearing a vascular neurologist say: "You really dodged a bullet. You should have died."

We've all experienced the pain of an unexpected crisis. When it happens, we scramble for shelter. We need something to cover us in the midst of the storm. The good news is that no matter what you're facing, God is present. He doesn't offer some sterile room as a shelter during your storms. *He* is the shelter. His presence with us is the only thing that can make sense of this life.

We need the presence of God as our shelter from the storm

WHAT DOES THE BIBLE SAY?

Psalm 23:1-6 *(HCSB)*

Acts 13:22

1 The LORD is my shepherd; there is nothing I lack.

2 He lets me lie down in green pastures; He leads me beside quiet waters.

3 He renews my life; He leads me along the right paths for His name's sake.

4 Even when I go through the darkest valley, I fear no danger, for You are with me; Your rod and Your staff— they comfort me.

5 You prepare a table before me in the presence of my enemies; You anoint my head with oil; my cup overflows.

6 Only goodness and faithful love will pursue me all the days of my life, and I will dwell in the house of the LORD as long as I live.

Key Words

Anoint (v. 5)—The Hebrew term denotes the pouring of perfumed oil on a guest's head (Luke 7:46). Psalm 23:5 describes God honoring David as His special guest.

Psalm 23:1-3

Psalm 23 has been a Christian favorite for centuries, but don't let your familiarity with these verses allow you to miss the vital truths they communicate. Specifically, David reminds us of three things God does for us as our Shepherd:

1. **He guides us.** Sheep aren't smart. They often wander aimlessly into one problem after another. That's why a shepherd's staff has a hook on one end—to haul sheep out of holes and ravines when they fall in. Likewise, God desires to help you navigate the tough places of life. When we're pulled off course or wander away, His presence guides us back onto "the right paths." The Shepherd isn't just interested in our rescue, but also our restoration.

2. **He provides for us.** A shepherd does more than just keep the sheep out of trouble; he also provides for their needs. God does the same for us. Because He is such a good Shepherd, we will lack nothing. In the midst of life's needs, sorrows, and grief, God provides perfectly for us.

3. **He renews us.** The psalm refers to green pastures (a place of rest) and still waters (a source of refreshment). It's only through God's presence in our lives that we can reach and enjoy these places of refreshment.

God is our Shepherd, which means we must submit to His care. When we try to take control, we only get ourselves deeper into trouble. It's like those Chinese finger traps—when you put your fingers in either end, any attempt to pull them out only causes the trap to tighten its grip. Similarly, when we struggle through life's difficulties in our own strength, we only tighten the grip that pain has on us.

God's presence brings about freedom, joy, and release from our struggle. When we decide to stop struggling and start trusting, we experience the relief and renewal we need.

> **What's your initial reaction to these verses?**
>
> QUESTION #2

GREEN PASTURES

Select the image that best represents your ideal situation for rest and refreshment.

☐   ☐   ☐

How can you intentionally seek God's presence during times of rest and refreshment?

God is active in revealing Himself to us.

God is our shepherd host

Psalm 23:2 pursue
Him look for us
God cares after us
Keeps us to live in
rest her on the still
water

"The right way to approach God is to stretch out our hands and ask of One who we know has the heart of a Father."

—DIETRICH BONHOEFFER

Psalm 23:4-5

What sometimes keeps us from recognizing God's presence?

QUESTION #3

As we move deeper into Psalm 23, we see that God protects us as our Shepherd. Because we know our weaknesses, it's easy to imagine ourselves as defenseless sheep wandering alone at midnight. We can't see the predators lurking in the shadows, but we sense their presence. We feel helpless and hopeless.

It's in these circumstances we need to remember the reality of God's protection. The shepherd's rod can be used to defend the sheep—and even as an offensive weapon. The staff can also be used to protect from harm. These images remind us that God is strong enough to protect us from any storm.

In addition to protecting us, God's presence gives us comfort. As the Scriptures say: "If God is for us, who is against us?" (Rom. 8:31). God Himself is the one who uses His power on our behalf when we face darkness and the predatory nature of this world.

Finally, God's presence brings about courage. Consider the dark valleys of life you must pass through. In many circumstances, there's really very little you can do to make things better. It's through prayer—through connecting with the presence of God in our lives—that we gain our courage.

▶ When the diagnosis comes, all you can do is take the medicine. And pray.

▶ When the company is headed toward a financial downturn, all you can do is work hard. And pray.

▶ When a relationship is on the verge of collapse, all you can do is love deeply. And pray.

How has God's presence in your life made you braver than you would be otherwise?

QUESTION #4

The imagery in verse 5 points to celebration. Specifically, the enemy is forced to watch as we celebrate. A huge banquet table is set before us. It's a time to feast and be glad because God is with us. We are the honored guests, and God has set us apart unto Himself. When we dine with the King, our cup will overflow with more of God's abundance than we can ever consume.

Psalm 23:6

Psalm 23 is comforting because of what it tells us about God and what He will do on our behalf. For many people, though, the real question isn't, "What will God do for me?" The real question is, "Will God love me?" Most of us are looking for love and acceptance.

The wonderful answer to that question is yes. God does love us! In many ways, that's the core message of Psalm 23.

David taught us through his psalm that God's goodness and faithful love will come after us—that they will be there for the rest of our lives. He was confident that God's "goodness and faithful love will pursue me all the days of my life."

▶ When we feel like temptation is pursuing us, God is more determined to win our hearts.

▶ When sorrows seem to be around every corner, the Lord is present to wipe our tears and win our hearts.

▶ When life is just plain hard and we don't know if we can overcome the pain, the Shepherd is present to guide us toward His love.

As long as you have breath in your lungs and a beating heart, you have the opportunity to embrace the love that longs to embrace you. God has a great desire for you: that you will live with Him. That's why He pursues you. **God desires to become your Shepherd and protect you in the deep, dark valleys of life.**

It's by His presence that you gain a sense of hope and courage. It's by His goodness that you dine at the King's table. Forever.

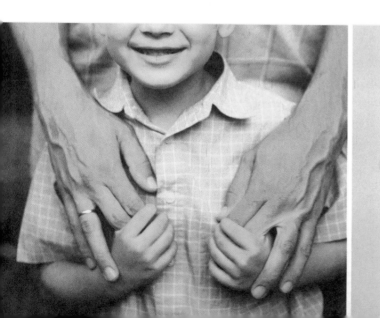

> *What does it mean to you that God's goodness and love pursue you?*
>
> QUESTION #5

LIVE IT OUT

Consider the following suggestions for living in the reality of God's presence and care:

▶ **Evaluate.** Identify circumstances in your life where you need protection, comfort, or care. Pray that God will help you be more sensitive to His presence in those situations.

▶ **Memorize.** Commit Psalm 23 to memory as an internal reminder of God's presence in your life.

▶ **Share.** Create printed cards or sheets with the words of Psalm 23. Share these with people who need the encouragement and support of God's presence.

My health problems were temporary. After treatment, I'm back to my normal self. But those experiences helped me take shelter in the presence of God. You can do the same. In the unexpected moments of life, let God's loving presence be your shelter.

Well-Placed Confidence

"I tell you, Peter," He said, "the rooster will not crow today until you deny three times that you know Me!" (Luke 22:34).

The words must have hung in the air, pointed and powerful. The disciples had just been arguing about who was to be the greatest in Jesus' kingdom. With Peter in the middle of the fray, Jesus' words cut to the heart.

To continue reading "Well-Placed Confidence" from *HomeLife* magazine, visit *BibleStudiesforLife.com/articles*.

My group's prayer requests

_____
_____
_____
_____
_____
_____
_____
_____
_____
_____
_____

My thoughts

SESSION 2

THE SHELTER OF GOD'S SALVATION

When did you first feel independent or on your own?

QUESTION #1

#BSFLsalvation

God Himself is my salvation.

THE BIBLE MEETS LIFE

Every person wishes for independence. It starts when we're toddlers stomping our feet because we think it will convince our parents to give us what we want. As older children, we think we can get our way through begging, pleading, and a bit of whining. Then the teenage years come along and our will kicks in even stronger. More and more we try to assert our own authority and make our own decisions.

But as much as we want to go it alone, we never reach a point where we don't need others. When I entered college, I suddenly realized how much I needed others I can rely on. Getting married, having children, and taking out a mortgage also helped me see how much I need others to help me.

For all of our efforts to gain independence in the world, there's one thing that holds us captive: our own sinful nature. While we're busy trying to gain our own place in the world, God has already given us His Son so that we can come back to the place He intended for us to be all along: secure and loved under the rightful rule of His kingdom.

WHAT DOES THE BIBLE SAY?

Psalm 27:1-6 *(HCSB)*

1 The LORD is my light and my salvation—whom should I fear? The LORD is the stronghold of my life—of whom should I be afraid?

2 When evildoers came against me to devour my flesh, my foes and my enemies stumbled and fell.

3 Though an army deploys against me, my heart is not afraid; though a war breaks out against me, still I am confident.

4 I have asked one thing from the LORD; it is what I desire: to dwell in the house of the LORD all the days of my life, gazing on the beauty of the LORD and seeking Him in His temple.

5 For He will conceal me in His shelter in the day of adversity; He will hide me under the cover of His tent; He will set me high on a rock.

6 Then my head will be high above my enemies around me; I will offer sacrifices in His tent with shouts of joy. I will sing and make music to the LORD.

Key Words

Stronghold (v. 1)—The Hebrew term denotes a place of refuge, along with the sense of strength, protection, and security that place of refuge provides.

Psalm 27:1

As David began this psalm, he identified God in three ways: his light, his salvation, and the stronghold of his life. God's presence in David's life in those ways meant something else was removed: his fear.

God can remove our fear as well. That's great news, since we all experience fear. It can come on our hearts like a sudden attack or build up slowly to harass us. Fear can come in the form of finances falling short, relationship problems, spiritual separation, and more.

But then along comes the Savior.

Psalm 27:1 gives us insight into how God Himself has provided salvation in such a way that it removes any fear we might have. When God shows up, He brings light. It's not just light to lead us down the trail so we can do our best to find Him. Rather, it's the light of salvation; He is the light. Jesus said in John 8:12: "I am the light of the world. Anyone who follows Me will never walk in the darkness but will have the light of life." The light God provides is His salvation that brings us back into a right relationship with Him. It eliminates the ultimate fear of eternal separation from God.

The reason we can trust this light—this salvation, this stronghold—is because it comes to us not as a thing, but as a Person. God doesn't have a treasure chest in heaven where He keeps forgiveness, life, and love stored away and hidden. Rather, God Himself is the salvation and light that we need. We gain salvation, light, forgiveness, love, and life because God gives Himself to us.

Because of this good news—the gospel—we can walk away from fear. That's why David asks two great rhetorical questions:

1. Whom should I fear?

2. Of whom should I be afraid?

We know the answer to these questions because God has arrived on the scene. In His presence, we have absolutely nothing to fear.

> *In what kinds of situations do you often feel afraid?*

QUESTION #2

Psalm 27:2-3

God's salvation doesn't just deal with the negative—with the removal of our fear. God's salvation also does something positive in our lives: it gives us confidence.

David highlighted the evildoers, foes, enemies, and an entire army who were deployed against him. Yet David's heart was not afraid; he was still confident. This great hoard of enemies confronting David began to fail, stumble, and fall. The only way such a thing was possible was because a greater Hero was on David's side. David had decided to take delight in the Lord. He trusted in God because he knew the Lord's power to be so much greater than his enemies.

As the Scriptures tell us, David trusted in his God, and "The LORD made David victorious wherever he went" (2 Sam. 8:14).

We deal with adversaries as well. They're pretty similar to the ones David faced. Financial problems, family stress, cultural craziness, and even wars around the world all plague us at one time or another. But just like David, we can gain confidence from our salvation, knowing that the enemies in our lives cannot overcome the victory God brings to us.

Our confidence in Christ doesn't mean we should lightly dismiss our foes. A quick trip through the Bible reminds us that we have a spiritual enemy who is real and must be faced and dealt with. But a review of the whole of Scripture also shows us that God is the main character of the story. And His story is also our story. He is active in saving us, and He wants us to enjoy a renewed relationship with Him.

> *What are the similarities and differences between self-confidence and confidence in God?*
>
> QUESTION #3

> *What are some positive and negative ways to face our foes?*
>
> QUESTION #4

Psalm 27:4-6

What's the "one thing" you want out of life? We all want something—some achievement or milestone that stands out in our minds:

▸ To fulfill a childhood dream

▸ To work in a certain career

▸ To find a spouse or an ideal family

Many of us look at this "one thing" as the answer to all of our problems and the hope for all of our joy. But consider someone who has achieved something similar to what you're hoping for. The question you have to ask is whether or not that person's accomplishments have brought real security.

David recognized that he could only find security through the presence of God. No human achievement, level of morality, or power-grab can deliver true security. Therefore, David decided to ask God for the one thing that would keep him secure: David wanted to dwell in God's presence. He wanted to be in a relationship with God so that he could gaze upon God's beauty.

When we ask for that same thing, we submit to the opportunity to live under God's grace. His beauty is the representation of His character, which is full of mercy and forgiveness. We all need shelter, and that's exactly what God provides to those who will trust in Him.

To give us this "one thing" we truly need—a home in God's presence—is why Jesus came to earth in the flesh. Jesus has done everything for our salvation and has given us everything we need to experience freedom from fear, confidence in victory over our enemies, and security through His presence.

That calls for one response from us: grateful and joyful worship.

How can we connect David's expressions of worship to our daily lives?

QUESTION #5

THE "ONE THING"

What's the "one thing" you're working toward right now—the goal, achievement, or milestone that has captured your attention in recent months?

What steps can you take to pursue this "one thing" in a way that glorifies God and reflects your ultimate need for salvation?

"Fallen man is not simply an imperfect creature who needs improvement. He is a rebel who must lay down his arms."

—C. S. LEWIS

LIVE IT OUT

Consider the following suggestions for responding to the truth that God Himself is your salvation:

▶ **Accept the Savior.** Trust Jesus Christ. Let His salvation give you the freedom, confidence, and security nothing else can.

▶ **Surrender your fears.** Make a list of circumstances that cause you to feel worried or afraid. Talk with God about your list through prayer, and then throw it away.

▶ **Share your faith.** Your friends and family have the same need for security and freedom from fear. Share with them the confidence and security you have found in Christ.

The gospel message that Jesus Christ died on the cross in our place for our sins is an amazing truth. He did not arrive on the earth simply to be a good example or to help make us the most moral people around. He is our light, our stronghold, and our salvation.

Excerpt: Stop Asking Jesus into Your Heart

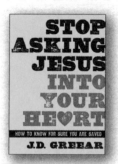

The young politician was genuinely learning to admire Jesus. He was fascinated by the message of this enigmatic, but wonderful, teacher. For many years he had been aware that something was missing from his life, and he was convinced he had finally found the missing piece. During an Easter service at the exciting, growing church he attended, he prayed to receive Jesus and was baptized the next week.

To continue reading this excerpt from *Stop Asking Jesus Into Your Heart,* by J. D. Greear, visit *BibleStudiesforLife.com/articles*.

My group's prayer requests

_____

_____

_____

_____

_____

_____

_____

_____

_____

_____

_____

My thoughts

SESSION 3

THE SHELTER OF GOD'S FORGIVENESS

Raspberry Pasta
Chocolate cake layered with chocolate mousse and raspberry jelly

BLACK FOREST PASTA
CHOCOLATE CAKE WITH VANILLA CREAM AND CHERRY FILLING

Greek Choc. Mousse
Two chocolate cakes with chocolate custard crème in the center

Vanilla Straw. Mousse
Two white cakes with strawberry crème in the center

Strawb

Napoleon

Fruit Tart
Pie Crust, Vanilla Custard, and fresh fruit on top

What "guilty pleasure" would be hard for you to give up?

#BSFLforgiveness

QUESTION #1

God's forgiveness brings restoration and joy.

THE BIBLE MEETS LIFE

You'd think the holidays would be an easy time to repair damaged relationships. After all, people are in a festive spirit, there's lots of food, and gifts are exchanged. Unfortunately, festive moods don't always translate into mending relational fences. We have this lingering hope that someone will make the first move to ask for forgiveness, but it doesn't seem to happen very often.

Forgiveness is a gift that's often hard to give. Why? Because it costs so much. The person doing the forgiving essentially forks over the whole payment; the main cost is letting go of the hurt and giving up the offense that was committed. Forgiveness means you walk away from the judge's bench and stand united with the guilty party.

Forgiveness was costly for God, too. Jesus took our punishment, and through Him, God offers us forgiveness. No matter what we've done, God forgives. What a wonderful gift He has given us! This sense of being forgiven is no mere emotion. Psalm 32 shows us that God's forgiveness moves us to a place of restoration and joy.

WHAT DOES THE BIBLE SAY?

Psalm 32:1-7 *(HCSB)*

1 How joyful is the one whose transgression is forgiven, whose sin is covered!

2 How joyful is the man the LORD does not charge with sin and in whose spirit is no deceit!

3 When I kept silent, my bones became brittle from my groaning all day long.

4 For day and night Your hand was heavy on me; my strength was drained as in the summer's heat.

5 Then I acknowledged my sin to You and did not conceal my iniquity. I said, "I will confess my transgressions to the LORD," and You took away the guilt of my sin.

6 Therefore let everyone who is faithful pray to You at a time that You may be found. When great floodwaters come, they will not reach him.

7 You are my hiding place; You protect me from trouble. You surround me with joyful shouts of deliverance.

Key Words

Hand was heavy (v. 4)—This phrase describes the weight of God's judgment, whether in a sinful conscience (Ps. 32:4) or in a physical affliction (1 Sam. 5:6,11).

Hiding place (v. 7)—The Hebrew term appears to mean something that hides or protects, like a shelter, covering, refuge, or hiding place (Ps. 18:11; 61:4; 91:1; 119:114).

Psalm 32:1-2

At the peak of David's reign as king over Israel, he blew it. He abused his power as king in order to sleep with a married woman named Bathsheba. Then, when she became pregnant, David took the unthinkable step of arranging for her husband's death during a battle as a desperate attempt to cover over his sin.

Fortunately, when God sent the prophet Nathan to confront David about his actions, the king repented. David confessed his wrongdoing and turned away from his sin (see 2 Sam. 12:1-14). Psalm 51 contains David's beautiful confession to God. And in Psalm 32 we see David's response to God's forgiveness: joy.

Joy can feel like a rare commodity in our lives. We're constantly looking for joy in things around us that are only temporary. The truth is that joy comes from something much more durable. Real joy arrives only in the form of Jesus. He is eternal, and He changes our lives rather than just smothering us with temporary gifts.

Remember that *happiness* can show up because the right chemicals in our brain combine or the right circumstances in our lives occur. *Joy* is not dependent on the temporary, but on the eternal. It's the response of our souls when we encounter God. **Joy comes when our sins are forgiven and our relationship with God is restored.**

David found joy when he laid down his deception (see verse 2). We must do the same in order to experience God's full forgiveness, but it's hard—especially when we deceive ourselves:

▶   My sin isn't *that* bad.

▶   I can stop whenever I want to.

▶   It's OK because no one really gets hurt.

Obviously, none of those statements are true. When we give up the self-deception of our rebellious lives, we can fully experience the joy of God's forgiveness.

> *What emotions do you experience when you receive forgiveness?*

QUESTION #2

Psalm 32:3-5

Have you ever kept quiet when you knew you needed to make a confession? Our silence eats away at us. David knew that feeling, too. During the time he refused to confess his sins, he felt like he was dying on the inside. He had the sense his bones were groaning and breaking. And it was constant—it was "day and night."

We come under the hand of God's conviction for the simple reason that He loves us. God wants us to confess our sins because confession brings about two major blessings. First, the sin itself is removed. David wrote in another psalm: "As far as the east is from the west, so far has He removed our transgressions from us" (Ps. 103:12). Second, the weight of conviction is released. Because the very sin that brought conviction is removed, God lifts the foreboding feeling that our life is wasting away.

Let me give you some practical suggestions for getting better at confessing sin:

▶ **Review the day.** Set aside a time each day to allow God's Spirit to survey your heart and show you any sins you've committed.

▶ **Find the motive behind the sin.** Oftentimes, there are deep-seated issues that cause us to commit particular sins. Allow God to show you the motive behind the action.

▶ **Get God's view about the issue.** Ask, "What has God said about this in the Bible?" True confession is agreeing with God about our actions and attitudes.

▶ **Be specific.** Don't generalize; instead, confess the individual and specific sins that the Spirit brings to mind.

▶ **Commit to repentance.** Completely turn from the sin with no desire to commit it again. Ask God for strength the next time you face temptation.

What's at stake when we hold on to unconfessed sin?

QUESTION **#3**

How would you describe the process of confessing sin to God?

QUESTION **#4**

Psalm 32:6-7

Picture this scene in your mind: because of your sin, judgment is coming toward you like a huge tsunami. You have no place to hide. But then everything suddenly goes dry. The water disappears. More than that, the world is put into the most perfect condition you've ever seen. It's a miracle!

When we experience God's forgiveness for our sin, that's exactly what it is—a miracle. When we confess our sin to God, He removes it completely and fully restores our relationship. Once we have confessed and been forgiven, then we can live in the restored relationship offered to us by God.

This happens as we recognize the nature of God and how He acts on our behalf. David identified three ways God cares for us:

1. **God is our "hiding place."** We need to find protection from the very judgment we deserve. God is fully justified to pronounce His judgment on us like an absolutely overwhelming flood. After our confession, however, God Himself steps in to be the place where we find shelter.

2. **God is our protection.** As we live in a restored relationship with God, we don't have to fear any trouble. He removes our fear and replaces it with His joy. We still face trouble, but we're never alone. God restores and protects.

3. **God surrounds us with celebration.** When others ask for our forgiveness, we often respond by forgiving in a begrudging way. Thankfully, God does nothing of the sort. He releases us from our guilt and begins celebrating.

It's the way of God to celebrate when what has been lost is found (see Luke 15). And we are what has been lost. How good it is to rest in the knowledge that Jesus brings us complete restoration and joy!

> *How have you experienced God's forgiveness as protection or a hiding place?*
>
> **QUESTION #5**

PICTURE IT

Because the psalms are poetic expressions, they're often packed with imagery and metaphor—Psalm 32 being no exception. Use the space below to sketch or illustrate one of the word pictures contained in Psalm 32:1-7.

"Love is the only force capable of transforming an enemy into a friend."

—MARTIN LUTHER KING, JR.

LIVE IT OUT

Consider the following suggestions for seeking joy through the blessing of God's forgiveness:

▶ **Confess.** Confess any sins that plague you. Turn from them, accept God's forgiveness, and make a plan with God about how to refuse their power in your life from this point forward.

▶ **Pray.** Pray for others who have not yet experienced the joy of God's forgiveness in salvation.

▶ **Forgive.** Offer forgiveness to someone who has wronged you. (*Note:* you can choose to forgive even if those who harm you never ask you to do so.)

We all want the gift of joy in this life. We usually grasp for joy in the same ways we find happiness—but that won't work. Instead, choose surrender as your path to joy. Surrender your will, let go of your sin, and relish the restoration that only God can bring.

Released from Hatred, Free to Forgive

From the time I was a little boy, I can remember my father relating his experiences as a Marine on the **USS Missouri.** *He took great pride in recalling his service to his country and considered it a privilege to play a part in protecting the freedom of all Americans.*

Although it was no secret how much he loved the United States, my father's hatred toward the Japanese was carefully camouflaged.

To continue reading "Released from Hatred, Free to Forgive" from *Mature Living* magazine, visit *BibleStudiesforLife.com/articles*.

My group's prayer requests

_____

_____

_____

_____

_____

_____

_____

_____

_____

_____

My thoughts

SESSION 4

THE SHELTER OF GOD'S ENCOURAGEMENT

When do you feel like singing the blues?

#BSFLencouragement

God encourages me when I feel overwhelmed.

THE BIBLE MEETS LIFE

Have you ever heard of acute post-holiday depression syndrome? Also known as the "January blues," people often experience this condition around New Year's Day. It's the emotional letdown you feel when the holidays didn't work out right—when you didn't have as much fun as you hoped. Sometimes we get the January blues because we actually experienced the chaos we secretly feared.

Even away from the holidays, it's common to feel overwhelmed. The craziness of preparing to have lots of fun can cause us to lose all sense of reason. Circumstances can completely overrun our lives.

We'll be looking at two psalms in this session. As we do, we'll find that even the psalmist had times when he was depressed and distressed. But God's presence can give us the encouragement we need. He will help us look above our circumstances.

As you explore these verses, look for the constant reminder to put our hope in God and worship Him in spite of what we face.

WHAT DOES THE BIBLE SAY?

Psalm 42:1-3,6-8; 43:3-5 (HCSB)

42:1 As a deer longs for streams of water, so I long for You, God.

2 I thirst for God, the living God. When can I come and appear before God?

3 My tears have been my food day and night, while all day long people say to me, "Where is your God?"

42:6 I am deeply depressed; therefore I remember You from the land of Jordan and the peaks of Hermon, from Mount Mizar.

7 Deep calls to deep in the roar of Your waterfalls; all Your breakers and Your billows have swept over me.

8 The LORD will send His faithful love by day; His song will be with me in the night—a prayer to the God of my life.

43:3 Send Your light and Your truth; let them lead me. Let them bring me to Your holy mountain, to Your dwelling place.

4 Then I will come to the altar of God, to God, my greatest joy. I will praise You with the lyre, God, my God.

5 Why am I so depressed? Why this turmoil within me? Put your hope in God, for I will still praise Him, my Savior and my God.

Key Words

Deep calls to deep (42:7)—This expression almost certainly denotes the powerful, rolling headwaters of the Jordan River that originate in northern Israel at the base of Mount Hermon.

Depressed (43:5)—The psalmist portrayed how he felt emotionally. He despaired of his circumstances, even as he asked for God's touch.

Psalm 42:1-3

These verses describe an intense longing for God. It's like that moment as a child when you became separated from your parents in a big store. You looked all around, but you didn't see them anywhere. You started to feel frantic. Suddenly it hit you that you might be lost—or worse, that you might be abandoned.

In a similar way, there are times when we wonder where God is. We want to believe He would never leave us as orphans, but we let life get in the way of our faith. Maybe you've experienced such a time. Maybe you feel abandoned even now.

It's during these times that we need to become like the deer described in verse 1. The deer isn't looking for a cool drink of water on a hot day. It's panting, longing, aching for the refreshment only water can bring. The deer is desperate for satisfaction.

That's how we should long for God's presence in our lives. We must thirst for God. We must decide that, even in the midst of overwhelming circumstances, we would rather have God's presence than anything else.

On that note, here are some ways to assess your spiritual desires:

> ▶ **Do I desire God Himself?** The psalmist wanted God above all else; his grief was profound when away from God's presence.

> ▶ **Do I desire Scripture?** The strength of your spiritual life is tied closely to your willingness to be a student of the Bible.

> ▶ **Do I desire to worship God?** Whatever receives your undivided attention is the focus of your worship. It takes an honest evaluation to determine what has your heart.

> ▶ **Do I feel sorrow away from God's presence?** When we are distant from God, we should have an unyielding desire to find Him quickly and be near Him again.

In your own words, how would you describe what the writer of the psalm experienced?

QUESTION #2

ASSESSMENT: SPIRITUAL DESIRES

Use the following questions to evaluate your spiritual desires. Circle the mark on the scale that corresponds with your answer to each question.

Your desire for God

How often do you intentionally seek to connect with God each day?

(rarely)   (regularly)

Your desire for Scripture

How much time do you spend reading the Bible during a typical week?

(zero hours)   (several hours)

Your desire to worship God

How confident do you feel in your ability to praise and worship God in a meaningful way?

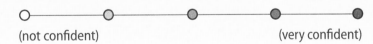

(not confident)   (very confident)

Psalm 42:6-8

Difficult times are all too real. The life we live on the earth is filled with hard, unexpected twists.

▶ The doctor calls with an unexpected diagnosis.

▶ Your boss announces you've been fired from your job.

▶ Your spouse tells you he or she doesn't love you anymore.

All these circumstances (and a thousand others) cause differing levels of spiritual depression. Make no mistake: depression is real, and it's awful. Even the psalmist admitted to it, and so should we.

To be "depressed" is a phrase that paints a picture for us. A physical "depression" is when something is pressed down below the surface—it's where a great force or weight has pushed hard against the normal plane of something flexible.

Spiritual, mental, or emotional depression is similar. It's when the weight of life overwhelms and presses down hard upon us. At that moment, when we feel stunned by life, we have a unique opportunity to remember the goodness of God. (*Note:* we all get discouraged at times, but that's not the same as ongoing or clinical depression. The roots and causes of clinical depression can be varied and diverse, and God also works through medicine and counseling.)

The psalmist leaned on his heritage of being a Hebrew. He sang about the promised land God had given His chosen people as a sign of His blessing. The Jordan River, Mount Hermon, and Mount Mizar were all recognizable landmarks to the Jewish people of his day. They were reminders that God never gives up on His promises.

Even the depressing circumstances themselves can remind us of God's goodness. Notice that the psalmist again uses water imagery to describe how the waterfalls, breakers, and billows that sweep over us are places where we can cry out to God. **We can learn to be thankful even for the difficulties of life because even those difficulties remind us of God's presence.**

> *What do the sounds and images in this passage communicate to you?*
>
> QUESTION #3

> *When you feel overwhelmed, what truths about God help you put one foot in front of the other?*
>
> QUESTION #4

Psalm 43:3-5

When we feel overwhelmed, we can ease our feelings of abandonment by remembering that God is still with us—but that's not the end. We must also move from that thirsty place of longing for God's presence to the blessing of enjoying a deep encounter with Him.

Ultimately, God's light and truth bring us into His presence. But we get there by faith in what God can do and what He reveals to us. Take a look at how the psalmist progressed:

▶ In 42:2, he referred to "the living God." This is a true statement, but it's broad and impersonal. It's the mental acknowledgement that there's only one true God.

▶ In 42:8, he moved to the phrase "the God of my life." This is the leap you have to make from knowing that God is there to believing that God is there *for you*.

▶ In 43:4, the psalmist called God "my greatest joy." As his view of God changed, so did his relationship with God—and so did his outlook on his own life and circumstances.

Depression is the sense that the world has got you down and intends to keep you down. But when God is near, we can turn to worship. As the psalmist approached the altar of God—the place of worship— he was able to find joy and reject depression.

Worship has the ability to turn our turmoil into hope. By focusing on the King of heaven, the craziness of life loses its grip on us. Whether in private or in a church service, worship guides us to the hope that is found when God is near. Additionally, worship helps us to declare a fundamental truth about our lives: that nothing rules over us but God—not even depression.

Instead, God is the true King of your life and the true Savior of your heart.

What are some ways to trust God when you don't know what to do?

QUESTION #5

LIVE IT OUT

How will you respond when hard times arrive? Consider the following suggestions to prepare yourself even now.

▶ **Choose worship.** Make the decision to actively worship God both in public and in private. Seek Him at all times so you'll know how to find Him when you're overwhelmed.

▶ **Encourage others.** Be intentional about speaking words of encouragement to friends, family, and coworkers this week.

▶ **Find help.** If you experience prolonged periods of depression, consider speaking with a close friend, pastor, or counselor about the deeper issues at the core of that struggle.

Whether or not you fight the January blues, you will feel overwhelmed at times—the waves of doubt will crash around you. But you don't have to drown. Depression will seek to embrace you, but you can choose the presence of God instead. Seek Him.

What to Do When Emotionally Under Siege

In recent years, Americans have experienced quite a bit of tragedy as a nation, and such events can leave us feeling emotionally drained. This global negativity only compounds the everyday, ordinary stresses life deals us.

My family has experienced its share of stress these last few years—perhaps yours has, too.

To continue reading "What to Do When Emotionally Under Siege" from *Mature Living* magazine, visit *BibleStudiesforLife.com/articles*.

My group's prayer requests

My thoughts

SESSION 5

THE SHELTER OF GOD'S PEACE

What have been your most successful New Year's resolutions?

QUESTION *#1*

#BSFLpeace

God is the source of peace in the midst of turmoil.

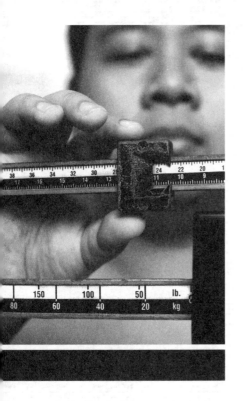

THE BIBLE MEETS LIFE

Do you make New Year's resolutions? If not, you still know which resolutions are most common: exercise, lose weight, spend more time with family, read more, watch less TV, and so on.

Have you ever thought about why people make such resolutions? One of the main reasons is a desire for a calmer life. We think, "If I can just live better, eat better, and be a better family member, then life will take on a new sense of harmony." Or, "If I can just gain a sense of balance or control, I will have a more peaceful life." But then life happens, and the idea of a better anything gets shot to pieces.

In reality, we don't need better resolutions. We need a *revolution*.

That's because resolutions are based on our ability to change our circumstances. A revolution is based on allowing a new authority to take charge and transform *us*. We need the revolutionary presence of God to bring to us what we cannot produce on our own. Peace, even in the midst of life's turmoil, is one of the revolutionary results of God's presence in our lives.

WHAT DOES THE BIBLE SAY?

Psalm 46:1-11 *(HCSB)*

1 God is our refuge and strength, a helper who is always found in times of trouble.

2 Therefore we will not be afraid, though the earth trembles and the mountains topple into the depths of the seas,

3 though its waters roar and foam and the mountains quake with its turmoil.

4 There is a river—its streams delight the city of God, the holy dwelling place of the Most High.

5 God is within her; she will not be toppled. God will help her when the morning dawns.

6 Nations rage, kingdoms topple; the earth melts when He lifts His voice.

7 The LORD of Hosts is with us; the God of Jacob is our stronghold.

8 Come, see the works of the LORD, who brings devastation on the earth.

9 He makes wars cease throughout the earth. He shatters bows and cuts spears to pieces; He burns up the chariots.

10 "Stop your fighting—and know that I am God, exalted among the nations, exalted on the earth."

11 Yahweh of Hosts is with us; the God of Jacob is our stronghold.

Key Words

Refuge (v. 1)—This Hebrew word literally means a "place of refuge," and can refer to a place of shelter for animals (Psalm 104:18) or humans (Job 24:8).

Stronghold (vv. 7,11)—Technically, this means a high point, like a cliff or rock outcropping (Isaiah 33:16) or high walls (25:12) that serve as a defensive position.

Yahweh of Hosts (v. 11)—One of the frequent names for God, this phrase is often translated "LORD Almighty" or "LORD of Hosts." The phrase proclaims the Lord's authority as King over Israel.

Psalm 46:1-3

Peace has all sorts of definitions. For some people, peace is the absence of open hostility toward *me*. For others, peace is only present when everyone lives in perfect harmony with one another.

My guess is that most of us would settle for something in the middle—something that applies to our everyday lives. Peace for me would mean fewer surprises at work, less stress in my family, and enough money to pay my bills. Is that too much to ask?

Psalm 46 points to a peace that goes way beyond simply overcoming the rut of daily routines. It's a change God brings that no calamity can overwhelm. How God does this is wrapped up in His very Person.

Notice how the psalmist began verse 1: "God is ..." Those might be the two most powerful words you can read, hear, or speak. Next, the psalmist described God with three distinct terms:

1. **Refuge.** When God is our refuge, we have a place to hide when life assaults us. When you feel battered and bruised and bullied, you can find a place of shelter with your Heavenly Father.

2. **Strength.** When life is hard, we're not forced to continue in our own power. Rather, God empowers us to take on life no matter what comes our way.

3. **Helper.** God is always there to help us. I love how personal this is. God, the Creator and Master of all things, helps me. No matter what I face, God is personally there to help.

The psalmist also described some pretty serious threats. We may not be physically facing an earthquake, mountains toppling into the sea, or the ocean flooding over us—but sometimes it feels like we are. We can't seem to get our footing. Stuff is crashing down all around us. Troubles show up like a flood against us. But the one who trusts in God does not have to be afraid.

> **Where do you go to experience peace?**
>
> QUESTION #2

> **God is our refuge, strength, and helper. Which of these three resonates with you right now?**
>
> QUESTION #3

WATER, WATER EVERYWHERE

The psalms are flooded with references to water in different forms. Write down any emotions you feel in connection with the images below. Examples are provided to help you get started.

Fear

Peace

Satisfaction

What emotions do you experience when you read Psalm 46?

"Trust the past to God's mercy, the present to God's love, and the future to God's providence."

—AUGUSTINE OF HIPPO

Psalm 46:4-7

In verses 2-3, the psalmist used tumultuous images of water: deep seas and roaring waters. In verse 4, he turned to the refreshing nature of water in a river or a stream. The Bible often refers to God's presence as a cool stream or a place where our thirst is satisfied (see Ps. 36:8; Isa. 48:18; John 4:3-14; Rev. 22:1). Yes, some images of water are terrifying—such as a roaring, foaming tidal wave—but nothing compares with God's presence. In the midst of raging waters, He is our calm stream.

One of my favorite movie battles takes place in *The Lord of the Rings: The Two Towers*. Taken from J.R.R. Tolkien's book, it's known as "The Battle of Helm's Deep." In the scene, a massive army of nasty, ogre-like creatures called Orcs attacks the men of Rohan in a lopsided battle. The humans are terribly outnumbered. It appears that the city of men will be wiped out. And then the hero arrives! Gandalf appears with additional forces and turns the tide of the battle. In the end, good wins out.

The Lord of the Rings is fiction, of course, but our lives can sometimes feel like the Battle of Helm's Deep. Good seems to get crushed into the ground. Good intentions, good work, and good morals are trampled by the "nations" that wage war against us. Yet even here, God isn't afraid—nor should we be. With the mere lifting of His voice, our enemies melt.

Words have enormous power. A word from our enemy can remove our sense of peace and replace it with anxiety in a split second. The voice of God, though, is far greater. When He speaks, His words confront those who oppose His peace. **When God speaks, all the enemies of peace are rendered null and void.**

> *How are you currently affected by the conflicts raging in today's culture?*

QUESTION #4

Psalm 46:8-11

In our war against the mayhem of life, God is completely unstoppable. God is not just a little bigger than our circumstances or the world. He is the all-powerful Lord and almighty Ruler over all things! He has the absolute ability to cease the roaring commotion in your heart.

It comes down to a choice. God has made peace possible between Himself and us. We were the enemies raging against His kingdom. We were the rebels making alliances with the chaos of the world. But God stands infinitely over and above all things. He is the true Hero of our battle, and He offers peace. But we must choose to trust Jesus rather than our stuff and our own willpower.

Yahweh is our stronghold (see v. 11). The name Yahweh is the ancient Hebrew name God used to reveal Himself as "the great I AM." It signals to us that He is eternal and needs nothing to sustain Him. Peace is ours because no nation, no act of humanity, and no self-imposed pain is greater than our God.

You need God's presence that brings peace in all kinds of situations:

▶ When family comes to visit.

▶ When the project at work is coming apart at the seams.

▶ When it's Saturday and your teenage daughter is an hour and a half late coming home—and she won't answer her phone.

▶ When you're enticed or tempted to sin for what seems like the millionth time.

▶ When problems must be solved, relationships must be mended, and chaos rages around you.

God's presence and peace is what you need, and God provides them. God is simply waiting for you to rush into His stronghold. The door is always open.

> **What steps can we take to seek God instead of our own ideas for peace?**
>
> QUESTION #5

LIVE IT OUT

Consider the following suggestions for allowing God to work in your life and bring peace:

▶ **Dwell in God's Word.** Read Psalm 46 daily for the next week. Choose one verse to memorize so you can remind yourself about God's power during times of turmoil.

▶ **Take a retreat.** Spend a significant portion of time alone in prayer and worship this week. Ask God to give you peace.

▶ **Get involved.** Identify a group or ministry that seeks to bring spiritual peace into the lives of people. Determine how you can help that cause.

You're going to face turmoil every day. That's not a pleasant reality, but it's true. Fortunately, you can actively choose to make a resolution in the face of turmoil. Be intentional to let God work a revolution in your life—a revolution of His peace and presence.

Tulips for Traci

I'm 42 years old and am recovering from bilateral mastectomies, a hysterectomy, and radiation treatments for breast cancer. Over my lifetime, I've watched my grandparents, cousins, uncles, and most recently my father pass away from one excruciating form of cancer or another—bone, brain, breast, pancreatic, and prostate. The stages and original prognoses may have differed, but the outcome never did.

To continue reading "Tulips for Traci" from *HomeLife* magazine, visit *BibleStudiesforLife.com/articles*.

My group's prayer requests

My thoughts

SESSION 6

THE SHELTER OF GOD'S PROTECTION

What causes fear in some people but not in you?

#BSFLprotection

God is my ultimate protection.

THE BIBLE MEETS LIFE

Know any "helicopter parents"? You've probably seen some. These are the moms and dads who hover obsessively over their children, afraid they might scrape a knee, need assistance, or get hurt feelings. Love is certainly a motive behind such behavior, but so is fear. And either way, the children will still fall down.

Many of us "hover" over ourselves, as well. We try to prevent any negative experiences from coming our way. Often we cross the line between protecting ourselves and living in fear.

How do we find that line? How do we balance between living in unhealthy fear and living with total disregard for the threats that challenge us? Such balance is gained through trust in God's protection. No matter what we face, we can know God is present.

Psalm 91 points us toward an awareness of God's presence. The psalmist helps us see that, while we don't need to live recklessly, we also don't need to live in fear. God is the great Hero of our story, and we can rely on Him for ultimate protection.

WHAT DOES THE BIBLE SAY?

Psalm 91:1-4,9-11,14-16 (HCSB)

1 The one who lives under the protection of the Most High dwells in the shadow of the Almighty.

2 I will say to the LORD, "My refuge and my fortress, my God, in whom I trust."

3 He Himself will deliver you from the hunter's net, from the destructive plague.

4 He will cover you with His feathers; you will take refuge under His wings. His faithfulness will be a protective shield.

9 Because you have made the LORD—my refuge, the Most High— your dwelling place,

10 no harm will come to you; no plague will come near your tent.

11 For He will give His angels orders concerning you, to protect you in all your ways.

14 Because he is lovingly devoted to Me, I will deliver him; I will protect him because he knows My name.

15 When he calls out to Me, I will answer him; I will be with him in trouble. I will rescue him and give him honor.

16 I will satisfy him with a long life and show him My salvation.

Key Words

Most High (v. 1)—The Most High (*Elyon*) is a divine title for God. It emphasizes the exalted character, supremacy, and omnipotence of the Lord.

The Almighty (v. 1)—The Almighty (*Shaddai*) is a divine title for the God of Israel who revealed Himself to the Patriarchs (Ex. 6:3). It refers to God's all-powerful nature.

Psalm 91:1-4

We think it was Benjamin Franklin who first said, "Nothing is certain except death and taxes." He made a good point. Finding something meaningful to count on in life often seems like a fool's errand. Jobs come and go. People let us down. Our stuff breaks. We even let ourselves down.

But then God enters the picture. Nothing in this world can compare with the strength and protection God gives us. He is certain!

One way we can begin to understand just how God works on our behalf is to investigate the names and titles He uses to reveal Himself. Notice these examples from verses 1-2:

1. **Most High.** No one is above God. He is the One who stands in the loftiest position. He is supreme.

2. **Almighty.** This is not just "stronger-than-the-next-guy" strength. God holds all of the power in all of creation throughout all of eternity.

3. **LORD.** This is the name that God used to reveal Himself to His chosen people. It is the covenant name Yahweh, which means "I AM." In other words, God is self-existent, self-sustaining, and eternal. He is the One who creates and holds everything else together.

When we see God in light of how He reveals Himself, counting on Him for protection suddenly becomes a lot easier.

Also notice God's hospitality in these verses. We're under His protection, in His shadow, in His fortress, and under His wing. The great God of the universe—who doesn't need me, you, or anyone else—does something completely unnecessary and perhaps unexpected: He welcomes us into His protective presence.

The ancient writer of this song was certain about God's ability to protect him in all kinds of circumstances. We must learn to trust Him in our lives as well.

> *What do the names and images in this passage reveal about God's character?*
>
> QUESTION #2

Psalm 91: 9-11

In the movie *The Wizard of Oz*, Dorothy, the Tin Man, and the Scarecrow were traveling down the Yellow Brick Road when the Tin Man explained the dangers that might lurk ahead. The three of them began to chant over and over again: "Lions and tigers and bears. Oh my!"

In verses 3-13, the psalmist painted his own picture of the dangers that lurk in the shadowy places of our lives: the hunter's net, the destructive plague, the terror of the night, the arrow that flies by day, the plague that stalks in darkness, the pestilence that ravages at noon, the lion, the cobra, and so on.

If that weren't enough, we often rehearse our own secret fears—both the real problems we face and the perceived dangers we fear may be lurking in the shadows. Physical pain. Mental stress. Emotional struggle. Financial worry.

If we're not careful, we'll find ourselves chanting our own version of "Lions and tigers and bears. Oh my!"

I don't say that to trivialize your problems. But the truth is you have Someone watching over you who is greater than those problems. **God's sovereignty means He can protect you in all things.**

God goes so far as to involve the very forces of heaven on your behalf "to protect you in all your ways." Our Heavenly Father is absolutely, positively certain you never will be in any circumstance in which He is not watching you, guarding you, and guiding you. You will run into problems, of course—but you won't be alone. God's kind control means His eye is on you.

> *How can we reconcile the reality of suffering with the truths in these verses?*

QUESTION #3

Psalm 91:14-16

God is fully able to protect us. But He places a decision in our laps—the decision to be devoted to Him or to rely on ourselves.

Recall the circumstances the psalmist recorded earlier about plagues, cobras, and the like (vv. 3-13). In the middle of all that, God does the most amazing things for us when we are "lovingly devoted" to Him: He overshadows the list of potential threats and problems with His own list of "I will" statements: "I will deliver him." "I will protect him." "I will answer him." "I will be with him." "I will rescue him." "I will satisfy him with a long life and show him My salvation."

Wow! But that's just the beginning of how God relates to you. In fact, He goes far beyond just preserving your existence:

> ▶ **God knows your name.** You are not anonymous to the King of the universe. He knows you personally (Isa. 49:16).

> ▶ **God answers when you call out to Him.** In the midst of the countless prayers lifted up before Him, God hears *your* prayer. And He listens (1 John 5:14-15).

> ▶ **God is right beside you when trouble appears.** The idea that God would leave you as an orphan is an outright lie. He never abandons His people (Josh. 1:9; Matt. 28:20).

God rescues and honors you. Most people in trouble would be happy just to be rescued and taken out of danger. But God replaces the hazards with a place of honor. God doesn't just want you sheltered; He wants you satisfied with eternal salvation (Eph. 2:1-9).

Best of all, God wants you to have an eternal relationship with Him through the power of Jesus' sacrifice for us. When you've made the decision to lovingly surrender to His grace and mercy, then the dangers, turmoil, and chaos of life lose their teeth. They become just more opportunities for God to show off how much He loves you.

> *How does our culture influence the way we view God's protection?*
>
> QUESTION #4

> *What responsibility do we have in being sheltered by God's protection?*
>
> QUESTION #5

GOD HEARS

The psalmists included confident prayers in their songs because they had confidence God heard them. God hears our prayers, as well. Therefore, use the space provided to write out a brief prayer—a quick cry to God about an issue that weighs heavily on your heart.

As you hear from God in the days to come, use the space below to record His answers to your prayer.

LIVE IT OUT

How will you express trust in God's protection? Consider the following suggestions:

▶ **Accept God's protection.** As you speak with God this week, actively accept His offer of protection.

▶ **Keep a journal.** Start a journal to record God's comforting work in your life. Take special note of the ways He protects you during difficult situations and cares for you over time.

▶ **Share the news.** Read Psalm 91 to a friend experiencing troubles. Share from your experience about the meaning of the psalm and how to trust God when the days get dark.

The lure of fearful self-preservation calls us to live helicopter lives, hovering over each day with a long list of "don'ts" and risks to avoid. God invites us instead to *do* something—to be lovingly devoted to Him and to trust Him completely.

Your Resurrection Year

Merryn had been expecting Emily's call. It was a routine call with the results of the latest blood test. She pressed the phone to her ear. "I'm afraid," Emily said quietly, "things have changed."

"What do you mean?" Merryn asked.

"Your pregnancy hormone levels have dropped significantly. I'm so sorry."

To continue reading "Your Resurrection Year" from *HomeLife* magazine, visit *BibleStudiesforLife.com/articles*.

My group's prayer requests

My thoughts

Storm Shelter: God's Embrace in the Psalms

It's wonderful to know that when we place ourselves in God's loving embrace, we can experience shelter in the midst of any downpour.

Christit

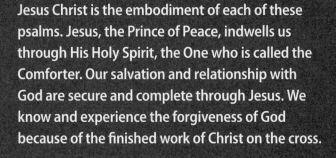

Jesus Christ is the embodiment of each of these psalms. Jesus, the Prince of Peace, indwells us through His Holy Spirit, the One who is called the Comforter. Our salvation and relationship with God are secure and complete through Jesus. We know and experience the forgiveness of God because of the finished work of Christ on the cross.

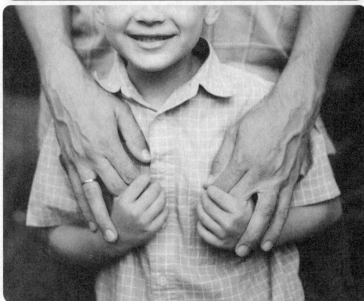

Community

God embraces us through our relationship with Him. As He indwells each of us, we experience God's presence, comfort, and encouragement. We are the body of Christ and we minister God's presence and help to one another.

Culture

Everyone looks for shelter from life's problems and downturns, but God is our only true shelter. As we experience difficulties, our trust in the presence and shelter of God gives testimony to the power and grace of God in our lives. As we see others in difficulty, we can point them to the shelter and protection only God can provide.

GENERAL INSTRUCTIONS

In order to make the most of this study and to ensure a richer group experience, it's recommended that all group participants read through the teaching and discussion content in full before each group meeting. As a leader, it is also a good idea for you to be familiar with this content and prepared to summarize it for your group members as you move through the material each week.

Each session of the Bible study is made up of three sections:

1. THE BIBLE MEETS LIFE.

An introduction to the theme of the session and its connection to everyday life, along with a brief overview of the primary Scripture text. This section also includes an icebreaker question or activity.

2. WHAT DOES THE BIBLE SAY?

This comprises the bulk of each session and includes the primary Scripture text along with explanations for key words and ideas within that text. This section also includes most of the content designed to produce and maintain discussion within the group.

3. LIVE IT OUT.

The final section focuses on application, using bulleted summary statements to answer the question, *So what?* As the leader, be prepared to challenge the group to apply what they learned during the discussion by transforming it into action throughout the week.

For group leaders, the *Storm Shelter* Leader Guide contains several features and tools designed to help you lead participants through the material provided.

QUESTION 1—ICEBREAKER

These opening questions and/or activities are designed to help participants transition into the study and begin engaging the primary themes to be discussed. Be sure everyone has a chance to speak, but maintain a low-pressure environment.

DISCUSSION QUESTIONS

Each "What Does the Bible Say?" section features at least four questions designed to spark discussion and interaction within your group. These questions encourage critical thinking, so be sure to allow a period of silence for participants to process the question and form an answer.

The *Storm Shelter* Leader Guide also contains follow-up questions and optional activities that may be helpful to your group, if time permits.

DVD CONTENT

Each video features Philip Nation discussing the primary themes found in the session. We recommend that you show this video in one of three places: (1) At the beginning of group time, (2) After the icebreaker, or (3) After a quick review and/or summary of "What Does the Bible Say?" A video summary is included as well. You may choose to use this summary as background preparation to help you guide the group.

The Leader Guide contains additional questions to help unpack the video and transition into the discussion. For a digital Leader Guide with commentary, see the "Leader Tools" folder on the DVD-ROM in your Leader Kit.

For helps on how to use *Bible Studies for Life*, tips on how to better lead groups, or additional ideas for leading, visit: **www.ministrygrid.com/web/BibleStudiesforLife.**

SESSION ONE: THE SHELTER OF GOD'S PRESENCE

The Point: God is with me no matter what I'm facing.

The Passage: Psalm 23:1-6

The Setting: David apparently composed this psalm in the midst of or reflecting back on a time when his enemies were close at hand and the outcome of the conflict was far from certain. The situation was severe enough that David could have feared for his life; instead, God's presence and goodness allowed him to say, "I fear no danger" (v. 4). This former shepherd could plainly see how the Great Shepherd guided, cared, and provided for him.

QUESTION 1: What is the biggest storm you've ever encountered?

> *Optional activity:* Help group members connect with the theme of this study by handing out an "emergency poncho" to each person. (These are available at most retail stores and cost between $1 and $2 each.) **Note:** If you have an adventurous group, encourage everyone to immerse themselves in the theme of the study by wearing the ponchos while discussing Question 1.

Video Summary: In this opening video message, Philip focuses on the passage for this week's session, Psalm 23. This psalm, written by David, is a song of praise and reflection. It helps us see the presence of God and apply that presence to every circumstance in life. God wants to be our shelter, our strong presence in all circumstances. He is our Shepherd and our Host. He wants to reveal Himself to us. He desires to protect us, and He comes for us.

WATCH THE DVD SEGMENT FOR SESSION 1, THEN USE THE FOLLOWING QUESTIONS AND DISCUSSION POINTS TO TRANSITION INTO THE STUDY.

- What do you think it means to truly run and hide in the presence of God?
- How does it make you feel to know that God is coming after you?

WHAT DOES THE BIBLE SAY?

ASK FOR A VOLUNTEER TO READ ALOUD PSALM 23:1-6.

Response: What's your initial reaction to these verses?

- What do you like about the text?
- What questions do you have about these verses?

TURN THE GROUP'S ATTENTION TO PSALM 23:1-3.

QUESTION 2: What's your initial reaction to these verses?

Because this is such a familiar passage of Scripture, encourage group members to also reflect on the ways they've encountered and benefited from these verses in the past.

> *Optional follow-up:* Which of the Shepherd's actions is most meaningful to you right now? Why?

> *Optional activity:* Direct group members to complete the activity "Green Pastures" on page 9. If time permits, ask for volunteers to share how they prefer to experience rest and refreshment.

MOVE TO PSALM 23:4-5.

QUESTION 3: What sometimes keeps us from recognizing God's presence?

This question is designed to help group members consider distractions that can get in the way of us recognizing God's presence in our lives and in situations we encounter. Answers will vary based on individual experiences.

Optional follow-up: What helps you recognize God's presence when you need it?

QUESTION 4: How has God's presence in your life made you braver than you would be otherwise?

This question will allow group members an opportunity to share personal stories as well as acknowledge and reflect on how their lives have been affected by God's presence.

Optional follow-up: How can we intentionally enjoy God's presence?

CONTINUE WITH PSALM 23:6.

QUESTION 5: What does it mean to you that God's goodness and love pursue you?

The emphasis of this question should be on the word *pursue*. Help group members engage the reality that God doesn't love us in a way that is passive or distant. He actively pursues us in His love for us.

Optional follow-up: What does God's pursuit of us teach us about pursuing others?

Note: The following question does not appear in the group member book. Use it in your group discussion as time allows.

QUESTION 6: How can we help one another feel more confident in God's love?

This question is associated with building biblical community. Helping one another draw from who God promises to be is indicative of the kind of community described in Acts 2. Belonging to redemptive community is an important aspect of living life with a secure future in God.

LIVE IT OUT

Encourage group members to consider the following suggestions for living in the reality of God's presence and care:

- **Evaluate.** Identify circumstances in your life where you need protection, comfort, or care. Pray that God will help you be more sensitive to His presence in those situations.

- **Memorize.** Commit Psalm 23 to memory as an internal reminder of God's presence in your life.

- **Share.** Create printed cards or sheets with the words of Psalm 23. Share these with people who need the encouragement and support of God's presence.

Challenge: We've all experienced the pain of an unexpected crisis. But no matter what we face, God is present. He is our shelter. Spend some time this week thinking back over times in your life when you have known this to be true. Consider journaling about those experiences so you can be easily reminded of them in times of doubt. In the unexpected moments of life, God's loving presence has been and always will be available to us.

Pray: Ask for prayer requests and ask group members to pray for the different requests as intercessors. As the leader, close this time by asking the Lord to help each of you remember that He will provide for you, no matter what you're facing. Thank Him for the privilege of experiencing His faithful love even in the worst storms of life.

The Point: God Himself is my salvation.

The Passage: Psalm 27:1-6

The Setting: Some Bible scholars believe Psalm 27 comes from the time of Absalom's rebellion when David had to flee Jerusalem. In any case, this portion of the psalm reflects David's great confidence in God and the high priority he placed on worshiping God in His house. Whether fleeing from Absalom or another threat, or securely entrenched in Jerusalem, David's great desire was to worship the Lord and gaze on His beauty "in His temple."

QUESTION 1: When did you first feel independent or on your own?

> *Optional activity:* We often attempt to manage our lives according to our own strength. As an object lesson, challenge group members to test that strength by holding their group member book in their left hand and raising their left arm until it's parallel with the floor. Set a goal to continue holding the book for three minutes without lowering their arm. If necessary, you can save time by combining this activity with Question 1.

Video Summary: In this video message Philip focuses on Psalm 27 and the God who wants to personally deliver salvation to us. God wants to be the real answer to all the circumstances of our lives. Many of us have decided that we want to be our own light, our own salvation, and our own stronghold. But at the end of the day, we need God to be these things—to provide what we can't possibly provide for ourselves. God wants to be our Hero who stays, the Hero who calls us home.

WATCH THE DVD SEGMENT FOR SESSION 2, THEN USE THE FOLLOWING QUESTIONS AND DISCUSSION POINTS TO TRANSITION INTO THE STUDY.

- Lots of things in this life promise fulfillment but don't deliver. What was the last thing you found yourself tempted to believe would fulfill?
- What makes you fearful when you consider trusting only God for your fulfillment, believing that He alone is enough?

WHAT DOES THE BIBLE SAY?

ASK FOR A VOLUNTEER TO READ ALOUD PSALM 27:1-6.

Response: What's your initial reaction to these verses?

- What questions do you have about these verses?
- What do you hope to gain from studying about the shelter of God's salvation?

TURN THE GROUP'S ATTENTION TO PSALM 27:1.

QUESTION 2: In what kinds of situations do you often feel afraid?

Identifying emotions and feelings in a person's life journey is important in moving them to understand God. Questions like this help us understand ourselves better, which, in turn, help us understand how God works in our lives.

> *Optional follow-up:* How has God recently been your Light or Stronghold?

MOVE TO PSALM 27:2-3.

QUESTION 3: What are the similarities and differences between self-confidence and confidence in God?

Group members may feel they are supposed to answer this question by focusing on the differences—that having confidence in God is good, therefore self-confidence is bad. Encourage them to think through the positive elements of self-confidence, including its connection to our confidence in God.

> *Optional follow-up:* How does confidence in your salvation affect how you face the dangers of life?

QUESTION 4: What are some positive and negative ways to face our foes?

We all deal with adversaries. Identifying how we have successfully and unsuccessfully dealt with them is the first step in gaining confidence that we're equipped to move forward in the truth that God is our salvation and only He can bring victory over our foes.

CONTINUE WITH PSALM 27:4-6.

QUESTION 5: How can we connect David's expressions of worship to our daily lives?

The question requires that group members interpret this Scripture passage for themselves as a way to move them toward life application.

> *Optional follow-up:* How is dependence on Christ an act of worship?

> *Optional activity:* Direct group members to complete the activity "The 'One Thing'" on page 21. If time allows, ask for volunteers to share their responses.

Note: The following question does not appear in the group member book. Use it in your group discussion as time allows.

QUESTION 6: What questions would you like to ask about the topic of salvation?

Hopefully group members will consider your group a safe place to ask questions they may have been reluctant to ask in the past. Be prepared to start this discussion yourself if group members seem hesitant. It's likely both believers and non-believers have or have had questions regarding salvation, but be sensitive to non-Christians who may be in the group.

> *Optional follow-up:* In what ways can having your own questions about salvation answered better prepare you to answer questions others may have?

LIVE IT OUT

Invite group members to consider the following suggestions for ways they can respond to the truth that God Himself is their salvation:

- **Accept the Savior.** Trust Jesus Christ. Let His salvation give you the freedom, confidence, and security nothing else can.
- **Surrender your fears.** Make a list of circumstances that cause you to feel worried or afraid. Talk with God about your list through prayer, and then throw the list away.
- **Share your faith.** Your friends and family have the same need for security and freedom from fear. Share with them the confidence and security you have found in Christ.

Challenge: Every person wishes for independence. More and more we try to assert our own authority and make our own decisions. But as much as we want to go it alone, we never reach a point where we don't need others. Ask the Lord to make you more aware this week of the times and situations in your life when you're still tempted to try to go it on your own. Remember that God has given us His Son so that we can come back to the place He intended for us to be all along: secure and loved under the rightful rule of His kingdom.

Pray: Ask for prayer requests and ask group members to pray for the different requests as intercessors. As the leader, close this time by committing the members of your group to the Lord and asking Him to help each of you remember who it is you ultimately depend on. Thank Him for all of the blessings included in your salvation, including the privilege of His presence.

SESSION THREE: THE SHELTER OF GOD'S FORGIVENESS

The Point: God's forgiveness brings restoration and joy.

The Passage: Psalm 32:1-7

The Setting: Despite being identified by God as "a man after my own heart" (Acts 13:22, NIV), David sinned in his affair with Bathsheba—and sinned again by attempting to cover up his illicit activity. God didn't fall for any of the cover up and sent Nathan to spotlight David's guilt. In Psalm 51, David poured out his heart in repentance over his sin and sought God's forgiveness. In Psalm 32, David rejoiced over the forgiveness he received.

QUESTION 1: What "guilty pleasure" would be hard for you to give up?

Remind group members that you're not asking them to discuss anything dark or overly personal. Examples of a "guilty pleasure" could include chocolate ice cream or a frivolous TV show.

> *Optional activity:* "The Bible Meets Life" section introduces the truth that our forgiveness was costly for God. As a bridge to that concept, print out pictures and descriptions of popular Christmas gifts. Pass the pictures around the group one at a time and encourage group members to guess the price of each gift.

Video Summary: This week Philip focuses on Psalm 32 as well as Psalm 51—David's prayer of confession. God doesn't keep score or expect us to make things up to Him when we're wrong. Instead He delights in restoring us. Psalm 32 gives us a portrait of the pain David experienced from his unconfessed sin. But later we get an opportunity to see the joy that can come when God forgives and restores. He wants to direct our steps. He wants to forgive us, restore us, and give us the greatest joy we can ever imagine.

WATCH THE DVD SEGMENT FOR SESSION 3, THEN USE THE FOLLOWING QUESTIONS AND DISCUSSION POINTS TO TRANSITION INTO THE STUDY.

- When was the last time you had to admit that you were wrong?

- What changed after you admitted you were wrong?

WHAT DOES THE BIBLE SAY?

ASK FOR A VOLUNTEER TO READ ALOUD PSALM 32:1-7.
Response: What's your initial reaction to these verses?

- What questions do you have about these verses?

- What new application do you hope to get from this passage?

TURN THE GROUP'S ATTENTION TO PSALM 32:1-2.

QUESTION 2: What emotions do you experience when you receive forgiveness?

Open this discussion by talking about the emotion David experienced and shared in these verses. Through the lens of this passage, group members will have an opportunity to share how forgiveness has made them feel.

Optional follow-up: What emotions do you experience when you extend forgiveness?

MOVE TO PSALM 32:3-5.

QUESTION 3: What's at stake when we hold on to unconfessed sin?

This question is designed to give group members an opportunity to consider the consequences of not confessing their sin and asking for forgiveness. Encourage them to consider not only how it affects them personally but also how it affects their relationship with God and even others.

Optional activity: Why does unconfessed sin eat away at a believer?

QUESTION 4: How would you describe the process of confessing sin to God?

Give group members an opportunity to share how they view the process of confession. Consider using the list of suggestions on page 29 as a beginning point for your discussion.

Optional follow-up: How would you explain the tension between being afraid to confess yet desiring the forgiveness we know it can bring?

CONTINUE WITH PSALM 32:6-7.

QUESTION 5: How have you experienced God's forgiveness as protection or a hiding place?

Sharing and storytelling represent great ways for growing as a group. This question creates an environment for sharing relative to the text.

Optional activity: Direct group members to complete the activity "Picture It" on page 31. If time permits, ask for volunteers to share their illustration.

Note: The following question does not appear in the group member book. Use it in your group discussion as time allows.

QUESTION 6: What steps can we take to celebrate our forgiveness in Christ?

This is an application question included so that the group can share their action steps. It promotes accountability and the need to act on biblical principles.

LIVE IT OUT

Encourage group members to consider the following ways they can experience joy through God's forgiveness:

- **Confess.** Confess any sins that plague you. Turn from them, accept God's forgiveness, and make a plan with God about how to refuse their power in your life from this point forward.

- **Pray.** Pray for others who have not yet experienced the joy of God's forgiveness in salvation.

- **Forgive.** Offer forgiveness to someone who has wronged you. (Note: You can choose to forgive even if those who harm you never ask you to do so.)

Challenge: Spend some extra time this week meditating on Psalm 32:1-7 and the truth that God's gift of forgiveness moves us to a place of restoration and joy. He has given us an amazing gift. And in forgiving someone who has wronged us, we can share that gift with another.

Pray: Ask for prayer requests and ask group members to pray for the different requests as intercessors. As the leader, close this time by asking the Holy Spirit to convict you and other group members this week regarding sins that need to be confessed. Profess your desire to live in the shelter of God's forgiveness.

SESSION FOUR: THE SHELTER OF GOD'S ENCOURAGEMENT

The Point: God encourages me when I feel overwhelmed.

The Passage: Psalm 42:1-3,6-8; 43:3-5

The Setting: The repeated refrain in Psalm 42:5,11 and 43:5 leads many Bible students to conclude that initially the two psalms were actually united as one. Whether that was ever the case or not, both psalms reflect that the composer was distressed and depressed over his inability to worship God on His holy mountain. He repeatedly reminded himself to put his hope in God and to praise God as the remedy for his depression.

QUESTION 1: When do you feel like singing the blues?

Remind group members that this is a light question intended only to break the ice for discussion. You aren't asking anyone to share deep secrets or confess anything uncomfortable.

> *Optional activity:* Lead your group in an exercise designed to remind them what it feels like to be overwhelmed. Gather together in a circle. As the leader, start by saying a letter of the alphabet out loud. Next, instruct the person on your right to repeat your letter and add a number. The next person should repeat both the letter and number, and then add another letter. Continue around the circle alternating letters and numbers until someone is unable to accurately recite the entire chain.

Video Summary: This week's session focuses on Psalms 42 and 43. The psalmist was confident he would again joyfully praise God, but he was also honest that he didn't feel that way at the moment. It's human nature for us to try to avoid grief at all costs. But we can cry out to God and be totally honest with Him about what we're feeling. He wants to be our source of encouragement. He wants to be the overriding desire of our hearts.

WATCH THE DVD SEGMENT FOR SESSION 4, THEN USE THE FOLLOWING QUESTIONS AND DISCUSSION POINTS TO TRANSITION INTO THE STUDY.

- Share a time in your life when God didn't abandon you in the midst of your circumstances.
- In what ways does recalling the times when God didn't abandon you help you when you begin to feel overwhelmed?

WHAT DOES THE BIBLE SAY?

ASK FOR A VOLUNTEER TO READ ALOUD PSALM 42:1-3,6-8; 43:3-5.

Response: What's your initial reaction to these verses?

- What do you like about the text?
- What new application do you hope to receive about how God encourages us when we feel overwhelmed?

TURN THE GROUP'S ATTENTION TO PSALM 42:1-3.

QUESTION 2: In your own words, how would you describe what the writer of the psalm experienced?

This question is designed to help group members actively engage the Scripture text and then interpret, in their own words, the expressions of the writer.

> *Optional follow-up:* What do you long for when you feel overwhelmed?

> *Optional activity:* Direct group members to complete the activity "Assessment: Spiritual Desires" on page 39.

MOVE TO PSALM 42:6-8.

QUESTION 3: What do the sounds and images in this passage communicate to you?

This question offers a great opportunity to engage group members who possess visual and/or auditory learning styles. Take advantage of this chance to explore the poetic nature of this psalm.

QUESTION 4: When you feel overwhelmed, what truths about God help you put one foot in front of the other?

This question requires group members to first get in touch with what circumstances cause them to feel overwhelmed and then apply the truth of Scripture to those emotions. Encourage them to search beyond the designated text for this session and find other applicable promises from God.

> *Optional follow-up:* How would you like to respond when trouble comes your way?

CONTINUE WITH PSALM 43:3-5.

QUESTION 5: What are some ways to trust God when you don't know what to do?

The foundation for answering this question was built in your discussion of truths about God in Question 4. Encourage group members to be specific with their answers. Also ask them to consider how their behavior reveals what they really believe about how trustworthy God is.

> *Optional follow-up:* When have you benefited from trusting God in the face of chaos or confusion?

Note: The following question does not appear in the group member book. Use it in your group discussion as time allows.

QUESTION 6: How has God encouraged you through worship?

This question invites members of the group to share their personal testimonies of how they have experienced God in their worship.

> *Optional follow-up:* In what ways could worship have a greater influence on your everyday life?

LIVE IT OUT

Invite group members to consider the following suggestions for how to prepare themselves for hard times:

- **Choose worship.** Make the decision to actively worship God both in public and in private. Seek Him at all times so you'll know how to find Him when you're overwhelmed.

- **Encourage others.** Be intentional about speaking words of encouragement to friends, family, and coworkers this week.

- **Find help.** If you experience prolonged periods of depression, consider speaking with a close friend, pastor, or counselor about the deeper issues at the core of that struggle.

Challenge: We all feel overwhelmed at times—the waves of doubt crash around us. But we don't have to drown. We can choose the presence of God instead. As you go about your normal routine this week, ask Him to help you be more intentional about placing your hope in Him and worshiping Him in spite of what you may face.

Pray: Ask for prayer requests and ask group members to pray for the different requests as intercessors. As the leader, close this time by asking the Lord to help each of you rest in His encouragement when you are feeling overwhelmed. Follow the psalmist's example—praise God for His goodness and encouragement in your life. Pray that everyone present will choose to remember God's character in times of crisis.

SESSION FIVE: THE SHELTER OF GOD'S PEACE

The Point: God is the source of peace in the midst of turmoil.

The Passage: Psalm 46:1-11

The Setting: Based on the inscription of this psalm, it's a choir anthem for congregational worship. Based on the content, it's somewhat akin to the hymn "A Mighty Fortress Is Our God" (which was inspired by this psalm) or "It Is Well with My Soul." The psalm celebrates God's great ability in all situations and identifies why His people can experience peace and security, specifically in times of trouble.

QUESTION 1: What have been your most successful New Year's resolutions?

Encourage group members to use their own definition of *successful* when answering this question.

> ***Optional activity:*** Help your group experience a moment of peace during the turmoil of the holiday season. Instruct group members to put away their phones and other portable devices, along with their group member books. Encourage everyone to close their eyes and simply rest—both physically and mentally—for two minutes. If time permits, unpack this experience by asking, "How would you describe what you experienced during the last two minutes?"

Video Summary: In this session Philip focuses on Psalm 46 and God's peace. Peace is a rare commodity in our culture today. The thought of being still and resting in the One who wants to be our peace instead of fighting for peace can be foreign. But God wants to be our Refuge, our Strength, our Helper. He can always be found in times of trouble. Not before or after the turmoil, but in the midst of the chaos. God is the One who can deliver true peace. And, as believers, we are the place He wants His peace to reside.

WATCH THE DVD SEGMENT FOR SESSION 5, THEN USE THE FOLLOWING QUESTIONS AND DISCUSSION POINTS TO TRANSITION INTO THE STUDY.

- What are the things you tend to cling to instead of God?

- On a scale of 1 to 10—1 being "I'm fighting for peace." and 10 being "I am able to be still and know that He is God."— how would you rate yourself? Explain your answer.

WHAT DOES THE BIBLE SAY?

ASK FOR A VOLUNTEER TO READ ALOUD PSALM 46:1-11.
Response: What's your initial reaction to these verses?

- What questions do you have about these verses?
- What new application do you hope to get from this passage?

TURN THE GROUP'S ATTENTION TO PSALM 46:1-3.
QUESTION 2: Where do you go to experience peace?

Encourage group members to resist any pressure to answer this question in an overly spiritual way.

Optional follow-up: How do you respond to the statement that peace is a change brought by God that no calamity can overwhelm?

QUESTION 3: God is our refuge, strength, and helper. Which of these three resonates with you right now?

Use this question as an opportunity to remind group members that there are no "correct" answers for most discussion questions. You're asking for their personal thoughts and ideas.

Optional follow-up: What can we learn from the images in these verses?

MOVE TO PSALM 46:4-7.
QUESTION 4: How are you currently affected by the conflicts raging in today's culture?

This question gives group members an opportunity to consciously connect how the things going on the world around them affect them internally. This is a good time to come back around to the point of this session—God is the source of peace in the midst of turmoil.

Optional activity: Direct group members to complete the activity "Water, Water Everywhere" on page 49. If time allows and members are comfortable, ask for volunteers to share their responses.

CONTINUE WITH PSALM 46:8-11.
QUESTION 5: What steps can we take to seek God instead of our own ideas for peace?

Your goal for this question is to help group members think through practical ideas for approaching God in times of turmoil rather than relying on their own solutions. Therefore, encourage them to move beyond the usual answers such as "pray," "read the Bible," and so on. Help them go deeper.

Note: The following question does not appear in the group member book. Use it in your group discussion as time allows.

QUESTION 6: Which "works of the Lord" remind you that He is your source of peace?

This question requires members of the group to first revisit verse 8 of the text in order to move toward life application.

Optional follow-up: What actions can you take this week to share your source of peace with others?

LIVE IT OUT

Encourage group members to consider the following suggestions for allowing God to work in their lives and bring peace:

- **Dwell in God's Word.** Read Psalm 46 daily for the next week. Choose one verse to memorize so you can remind yourself about God's power during times of turmoil.

- **Take a retreat.** Spend a significant portion of time alone in prayer and worship this week. Ask God to give you peace.

- **Get involved.** Identify a group or ministry that seeks to bring spiritual peace into the lives of people. Determine how you can help that cause.

Challenge: Fill in the blank: "I could have some peace in my life if it weren't for _____." Whether a minor irritant or something that causes great turmoil, we can all complete that sentence. We're going to face turmoil every day. This week allow God to bring you a peace you can't produce in your own life—a peace that doesn't come from circumstances, situations, people, places, or things. A peace that's more than worth loosening your grip for.

Pray: Ask for prayer requests and ask group members to pray for the different requests as intercessors. As the leader, close this time by proclaiming with the psalmist that "God is our refuge and strength, a helper who is always found in times of trouble" (Psalm 46:1). Ask again that you and your group members would experience peace as you trust in God's goodness and power in the days to come.

SESSION SIX: THE SHELTER OF GOD'S PROTECTION

The Point: God is my ultimate protection.

The Passage: Psalm 91:1-4,9-11,14-16

The Setting: The psalmist celebrated the protection of the Lord throughout Psalm 91. The psalm has no inscription and can be associated with no particular time. Thus, its scope and timelessness are highlighted—any and every follower of "the Most High" can rely on "the Almighty" for protection. The psalm moves from first person testimony to second person exhortation to God Himself declaring the shelter He will provide.

QUESTION 1: What causes fear in some people but not in you?

Optional activity: To continue with the theme of God's protection being greater than self-protection, bring several magazines and/or newspapers to the group meeting—one per group member would be ideal. As you distribute the periodicals, instruct group members to search for advertisements and other content that promote or proclaim our ability to protect ourselves. These can include medical protection, financial protection, emotional protection, and so on. Allow 3-5 minutes for group members to search, and then ask for volunteers to share what they found.

Video Summary: In this last session Philip talks about Psalm 91 and the protection of God. Through a series of "I will" statements, God explains to us the shelter He will provide. Everyday life can be really tough—physically hard and emotionally taxing. But as believers we can know that we're under God's care forever. God is faithful and He is sovereign, and He offers Himself as our ultimate protection.

WATCH THE DVD SEGMENT FOR SESSION 6, THEN USE THE FOLLOWING QUESTIONS AND DISCUSSION POINTS TO TRANSITION INTO THE STUDY.

- What does the word *protection* mean to you?

- If you were able to completely trust in God's protection, what would be different in your life?

WHAT DOES THE BIBLE SAY?

ASK FOR A VOLUNTEER TO READ ALOUD PSALM 91:1-4,9-11,14-16.
Response: What's your initial reaction to these verses?

- What questions do you have about trusting God for your protection?

- What new application do you hope to get from this passage?

TURN THE GROUP'S ATTENTION TO PSALM 91:1-4.
QUESTION 2: What do the names and images in this passage reveal about God's character?

This question is designed to help group members connect what the text says with what it tells us about who God is. Consider being prepared with some additional information on God's names.

Optional follow-up: How has God protected you?

MOVE TO PSALM 91:9-11.
QUESTION 3: How can we reconcile the reality of suffering with the truths in these verses?

The so-called "problem of evil" has been a topic of discussion and debate for centuries. Therefore, don't feel like your group needs to arrive at a definite conclusion in a matter of minutes. Encourage group members to wrestle with the tension between the reality of suffering and the goodness of God—and then conclude by reinforcing the point of this session: "God is our ultimate source of protection" whether we experience suffering or not.

Optional follow-up: What does it mean to make God your dwelling place?

CONTINUE WITH PSALM 91:14-16.
QUESTION 4: How does our culture influence the way we view God's protection?

The goal here is to help group members consider how modern culture has influenced our beliefs on what it means to be protected—superheroes, police officers, vigilantes, and more—and how those beliefs influence our understanding of God's promises to protect us.

Optional follow-up: How have your experiences in the church influenced your views on God's protection?

QUESTION 5: What responsibility do we have in being sheltered by God's protection?

This question is intended to help group members make the connection between what God promises to do for us and our responsibility in positioning ourselves (through surrender) to receive His protection.

Optional activity: Encourage group members to complete the activity "God Hears" on page 61.

Note: The following question does not appear in the group member book. Use it in your group discussion as time allows.

QUESTION 6: How will we support one another in our devotion to God?

This is an application question designed to promote accountability and biblical community. Note that this question asks about actions you will take as a group, not as individuals.

LIVE IT OUT

Encourage group members to consider the following suggestions for how they can express trust in God's protection:

- **Accept God's protection.** As you speak with God this week, actively accept His offer of protection.

- **Keep a journal.** Start a journal to record God's comforting work in your life. Take special note of the ways He protects you during difficult situations and cares for you over time.

- **Share the news.** Read Psalm 91 to a friend experiencing troubles. Share from your experience about the meaning of the psalm and how to trust God when the days get dark.

Challenge: Psalm 91 points us toward an awareness of God's presence. While we don't need to live recklessly, we also don't need to live in fear. We can rely on God for ultimate protection. Spend some time this week researching other passages of Scripture that promise us we will never be abandoned. Consider posting some of the verses in places where you will see them often and be reminded of God's promises to you.

Pray: As the leader, close this final session of *Storm Shelter* in prayer. Ask the Lord to help each of you as you move forward to discover or rediscover the only One who can truly shelter us. Conclude by echoing the words of Psalm 91:2, "I will say to the Lord, 'My refuge and my fortress, my God, in whom I trust.'"

Note: If you haven't discussed it earlier, decide as a group whether or not you plan to continue to meet together and, if so, what Bible study options you would like to pursue. Visit *LifeWay.com/smallgroups* for help, or if you would like more studies like this one, visit *biblestudiesforlife.com/smallgroups.*

WHERE THE BIBLE MEETS LIFE

Bible Studies for Life™ will help you know Christ, live in community, and impact the world around you. If you enjoyed this study, be sure and check out these other available titles.* Six sessions each.

Pressure Points *by Chip Henderson*

When Relationships Collide *by Ron Edmondson*

Do Over: Experience New Life in Christ *by Ben Mandrell*

Honest to God: Real Questions People Ask *by Robert Jeffress*

Let Hope In *by Pete Wilson*

Productive: Finding Joy in What We Do *by Ronnie and Nick Floyd*

Connected: My Life in the Church *by Thom S. Rainer*

Resilient Faith: Standing Strong in the Midst of Suffering *by Mary Jo Sharp*

Beyond Belief: Exploring the Character of God *by Freddy Cardoza*

Overcome: Living Beyond Your Circumstances *by Alex Himaya*

Storm Shelter: God's Embrace in the Psalms *by Philip Nation*

Ready: Ministering to Those in Crisis *by Chip Ingram*

If your group meets regularly, you might consider Bible Studies for Life as an ongoing series. Available for your entire church—kids, students, and adults—it's a format that will be a more affordable option over time. And you can jump in anytime. For more information, visit **biblestudiesforlife.com**.

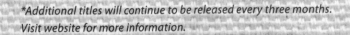

biblestudiesforlife.com/smallgroups
800.458.2772 | LifeWay Christian Stores

*Additional titles will continue to be released every three months.
Visit website for more information.*